A Crabtree Roots Book
Un libro de Las Raíces de Crabtree

FARM ANIMAL FRIENDS
Animales de granja amistosos

HORSES
CABALLOS

AMY CULLIFORD
SANTIAGO OCHOA

Crabtree Publishing
crabtreebooks.com

T0019816

School-to-Home Support for Caregivers and Teachers

This book helps children grow by letting them practice reading. Here are a few guiding questions to help the reader with building his or her comprehension skills. Possible answers appear here in red.

Before Reading:

• What do I think this book is about?
  - *This book is about horses.*
  - *This book is about horses on farms.*

• What do I want to learn about this topic?
  - *I want to learn what horses eat.*
  - *I want to learn what colors a horse can be.*

During Reading:

• I wonder why...
  - *I wonder why people ride horses.*
  - *I wonder why some horses are different colors.*

• What have I learned so far?
  - *I have learned that horses drink water.*
  - *I have learned that horses like to run.*

After Reading:

• What details did I learn about this topic?
  - *I have learned that horses eat grass.*
  - *I have learned that horses like to jump.*

• Read the book again and look for the vocabulary words.
  - *I see the word **drink** on page 6 and the word **grass** on page 8. The other vocabulary words are found on page 14.*

This is a **horse**.

Este es un **caballo**.

Horses can be black, white, or brown.

Los caballos pueden ser negros, blancos o cafés.

All horses **drink** water.

Todos los caballos **toman** agua.

All horses eat **grass**.

Todos los caballos comen **hierba**.

People can ride horses.

La gente puede montar a caballo.

All horses like to run, jump, and play!

¡A todos los caballos les gusta correr, saltar y jugar!

Words to Know
Palabras para aprender

drink
toman

grass
hierba

horse
caballo

31 Words

This is a **horse**.

Horses can be black, white, or brown.

All horses **drink** water.

All horses eat **grass**.

People can ride horses.

All horses like to run, jump, and play!

38 palabras

Este es un **caballo**.

Los caballos pueden ser negros, blancos o cafés.

Todos los caballos **toman** agua.

Todos los caballos comen **hierba**.

La gente puede montar a caballo.

A todos los caballos les gusta correr, saltar y jugar.

FARM ANIMAL FRIENDS
Animales de granja amistosos

HORSES
CABALLOS

Written by: Amy Culliford

Designed by: Rhea Wallace

Series Development: James Earley

Proofreader: Kathy Middleton

Educational Consultant: Christina Lemke M.Ed.

Photographs:
Shutterstock: Henk Vrieselaar: cover (tl); Jesus Cervantes: cover (tr);
   Barry Fowler: cover (b); Kent Weakley: p. 1; James Kirkikis: p. 3, 14;
   Lillac: p. 4-5; Andrej Kubik: p. 7, 14; Sheeval: p. 9, 14; RMC42: p. 11;
   pirita: p. 12

Crabtree Publishing

crabtreebooks.com   800-387-7650

Printed in Canada/042023/CPC20230419

Published in Canada
Crabtree Publishing
616 Welland Ave.
St. Catharines, Ontario
L2M 5V6

Published in the United States
Crabtree Publishing
347 Fifth Avenue,
Suite 1402-145
New York, NY, 10016

Library and Archives Canada Cataloguing in Publication
Available at the Library and Archives Canada

Library of Congress Cataloging-in-Publication Data
Available at the Library of Congress

Paperback: 9781039624467
Ebook: 9781039625303
Epub: 9781039624887

I CAN MAKE SET

I Can Make
TWELVE

CHRISTINA EA[RLEY]

A Crabtree Roots Book

Crabtree Publishing
crabtreebooks.com

School-to-Home Support for Caregivers and Teachers

This book helps children grow by letting them practice reading. Here are a few guiding questions to help the reader with building his or her comprehension skills. Possible answers appear here in red.

Before Reading:

• What do I think this book is about?
  - *I think this book is about making a group of twelve.*
  - *I think this book is about adding to twelve.*

• What do I want to learn about this topic?
  - *I want to learn how to add to twelve.*
  - *I want to learn ways to make twelve.*

During Reading:

• I wonder why...
  - *I wonder why one and eleven make twelve.*
  - *I wonder why two plus ten is twelve.*

• What have I learned so far?
  - *I have learned three and nine make twelve.*
  - *I have learned five and seven make twelve.*

After Reading:

• What details did I learn about this topic?
  - *I have learned that four plus eight equals twelve.*
  - *I have learned that six plus six equals twelve.*

• Read the book again and look for the vocabulary words.
  - *I see the word **plus** on page 6 and the word **equals** on page 9. The other vocabulary word is found on page 14.*

$$1+11=12$$

$$2+10=12$$

$$9+3=12$$

$$8+4=12$$

$$7+5=12$$

$$6+6=12$$

I can add to make the number twelve.

One and eleven
make twelve.

1

+

11

Two **plus** ten
is twelve.

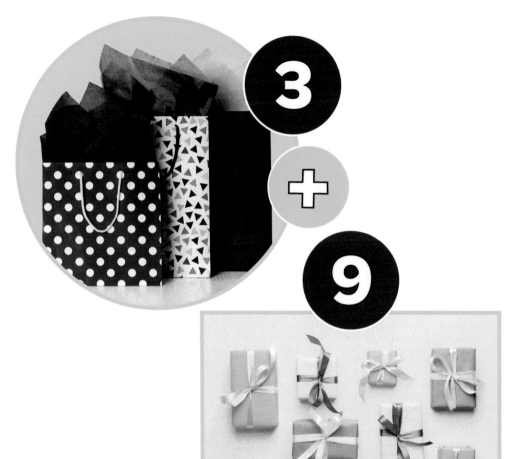

Three and nine
make twelve.

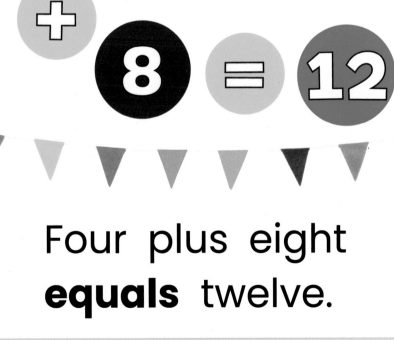

Four plus eight
equals twelve.

Five and seven
make twelve.

6 + 6 = 12

Six plus six
equals twelve.

There are many ways to make twelve at a **party**.

Word List
Sight Words

and	is	the
are	make	there
at	many	three
can	nine	to
eleven	one	twelve
four	six	two
I	ten	ways

Words to Know

equals

party

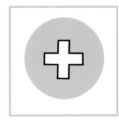

plus

48 Words

I can add to make the number twelve.

One and eleven make twelve.

Two **plus** ten is twelve.

Three and nine make twelve.

Four plus eight **equals** twelve.

Five and seven make twelve.

Six plus six equals twelve.

There are many ways to make twelve at a **party**.

I CAN MAKE SETS

I Can Make
TWELVE

Written by: Christina Earley

Designed by: Rhea Wallace

Series Development: James Earley

Proofreader: Janine Deschenes

Educational Consultant: Marie Lemke M.Ed.

Photographs:
Shutterstock: Rybalchenko: cover, p. 1; Dmitry Zimin: p.3; Ruth Black: p. 5(top); Africa Studio: p. 5(bottom); Andrei Kuzmik: p. 7(top); Yeti Studio: p. 7(bottom); New Africa: p. 8(top); Pixel-Shot: p. 8(bottom); yukihipo; p. 9(top); hans.slegers: p. 9(bottom); HomeStudio: p. 10(top); Holiday. Photo.Top: p. 10(bottom); Joe Belanger: p. 11(top); robert_s: p. 11(bottom; Lopolo: p. 13

Crabtree Publishing

crabtreebooks.com   800-387-7650
Copyright © 2023 Crabtree Publishing
All rights reserved. No part of this publication may be reproduced, stored in a retrieval system or be transmitted in any form or by any means, electronic, mechanical, photocopying, recording, or otherwise, without the prior written permission of Crabtree Publishing Company.

Published in Canada
Crabtree Publishing
616 Welland Ave.
St. Catharines,
Ontario L2M 5V6

Published in the United States
Crabtree Publishing
347 Fifth Avenue,
Suite 1402-145
New York, NY, 10016

Printed in Canada/062022/CPC20220609

Library and Archives Canada Cataloguing in Publication
Title: I can make twelve / Christina Earley.
Other titles: Twelve
Names: Earley, Christina, author.
Description: Series statement: I can make sets | "A Crabtree roots book".
Identifiers: Canadiana (print) 20210195215 |
    Canadiana (ebook) 20210195223 |
    ISBN 9781427156648 (hardcover) |
    ISBN 9781427156709 (softcover) |
    ISBN 9781427156761 (HTML) |
    ISBN 9781427156822 (EPUB) |
    ISBN 9781427156884 (read-along ebook)
Subjects: LCSH: Addition—Juvenile literature. |
    LCSH: Mathematics—Juvenile literature.
Classification: LCC QA115 .E275 2022 | DDC j513.2/11—dc23

Library of Congress Cataloging-in-Publication Data
Names: Earley, Christina, author.
Title: I can make twelve / Christina Earley.
Description: New York, NY : Crabtree Publishing Company, [2022] | Series: I can make sets - a Cabtree roots book | Includes index.
Identifiers: LCCN 2021017714 (print) |
    LCCN 2021017715 (ebook) |
    ISBN 9781427156648 (hardcover) |
    ISBN 9781427156709 (paperback) |
    ISBN 9781427156761 (ebook) |
    ISBN 9781427156822 (epub) |
    ISBN 9781427156884
Subjects: LCSH: Addition--Juvenile literature. | Mathematics--Juvenile literature.
Classification: LCC QA115 .E2717 2022 (print) | LCC QA115 (ebook) | DDC 513.2/11--dc23
LC record available at https://lccn.loc.gov/2021017714
LC ebook record available at https://lccn.loc.gov/2021017715